EVERSLEEP

THE BEAUTY OF DARK SILENCE

ALEXANDER BENTLEY

Printed in the United States of America

First Printing, 2017

ISBN 978-0692923139

SOSII PRESS

Sun City, Arizona

To the best of the publisher's and author's knowledge, all
illustrations used in this book are of the public domain and do
not require attribution. If you are the original artist of an
illustration, you may contact the publisher to receive proper
credit in a future printing or to contest its inclusion.

The Fell Types are digitally reproduced by Igino Marini.
www.iginomarini.com

Dedicated to
Chester Bennington
(March 20, 1976 – July 20, 2017)

GREY DAZE
LINKIN PARK
DEAD BY SUNRISE
STONE TEMPLE PILOTS

(Singer & Songwriter)

You were a passionate artist and tortured soul –
a voice of inspiration that gave me a reason
to fight my own demons during dark days.

I'm sorry nobody could save you.

Love,
A.B.

"WHEN it most closely allies itself to BEAUTY:
the death, then, of a beautiful woman is, unquestionably,
the most poetical topic in the world — and equally is it
beyond doubt that the lips best suited for such topic
are those of a bereaved lover." — EDGAR ALLAN POE

this is a story
of a boy
and a girl
and the tragedy
of their love.

Where I Go

it's sad i escaped
　　　into this dark oblivion,
　　　where i go, please don't follow.

for all my self torturous sins,
　　　this pain has left me hollow.

follow me if you dare,
　　　but where you go
　　　you cannot stare.

for all my demons
　　　will haunt your mind
　　　until the end of time

INTO THE SEA

into the sea
of monsters
i plunged
to find myself
and face
my demons

when i emerged
from haunted waters
i learned
the reason
of my curse.

i write to redeem my soul.

X-RAY VISION

i looked into myself
with X-Ray vision,
penetrating
all the layers,
deep down into my core.
i was disgusted
with what i saw
and what i saw was that
something dark lurks within.

What Is This Darkness?

i look beyond the light into the black mirror
i feel like there's something dark inside me —
festering, waiting to show its ugly head again.

i'm not sure when it found its way within,
but i know it's been there forever and a day —
waiting, echoing deep within the membrane.

if i could only find that moment it came to be
i might be able to root out the darkness —
and heal my withering, diminished soul.

The Beauty of Dark Silence

the slumber of death is alluring
it gives us pause, a chance to rest
it's darkness touched me today

as i was on the edge of oblivion,
i felt the Dark Silence wrap
it's arms around my soul

it wanted me to go with it
to go to the abode where
nobody returns from

but it couldn't have me quite yet
and because of this, it touched me
in a way where i carried back
something from the other side

it took a tiny bit of my soul
and in its place it put a mark
to plug up the tiny hole
it left behind in the dark

this dark night of my fainting soul
again, will i ever be whole?

Fortress

my pain: a fortress!

protected from intruders;
isolated from the enemy.

but little did i know,
the enemy was already
within these walls.

i return to madness,
like it's a long lost season
i've been missing.

EVERYDAY VICES

our everyday vices
    lead us into
    the outer reaches
    of sin.

further and further
    we must go
    until our faces
    are painted
    blood red.

turn DEATH's key,
    skull and bones,
    the price we pay
    for our sins.

like a bad book
    we read
    that never
    comes to
    its end.

POISON

there is poison
    in the heart of man,

shattered dreams
    while holding hands.

glitter on chapped skin;
    did it for the glam,

find me in the rabbit hole;
    i am what i am.

do you hear it —
    dark whispers
    in the heart of man?

HUNGER

there is a hunger
inside all of us
that must be fed.

we can eat
the rotting
carcasses
of the dead
or consume
the energy of
the living.

it is this hunger
that drives all men
crazy.

CURRENCY

the currency
    of dead bodies
    are the cost of
    the OLD MEN's wars.

bleeding veins
    pour me out, gushing —
    winding down streets
    to settle a score.

a dead philosophy
    of barbaric extremes
    bleeding the living
    for a nation's pride.

like thieves,
    we, little children,
    under cover of night
    find a way to hide.

Mostly Forgotten

we are mostly forgotten, but not gone
for our dreams bleed into more vivid dreams
and our seeds are planted in sunken soil
our plants do not grow; they just spoil

but no one would know, because
we are mostly forgotten.

A DESERTED SPACE

the long deserted space,
abandoned a long time ago.
never could i fill the void
with my ramblings of noise.

even as my heart beat
a triumphant beat of joy,
down the winding street
where my aching bones
now go to lay.

to think as a kid
this was the place
where i'd go to play.

but those times
are long gone,
here i am —
here is where
i lay.

GHOST IN THE DESERT

my name is NEVER MORE,
a ghost in the desert,
a phantom with a purpose,
a seeker of truth and justice,
encrypted by the shadows,
hidden inside the light of the sun —
i am the RAVEN's watchful eye!

A NEW REALITY

there's a break in reality,
a crack in the clay pot
where the tree of life sits,
soil seeping through,
water turned brown —
a beautiful sludge,
the holiest of names
transformed into
mud.

TANGLED DESTRUCTION

tangled
in a web
of destruction
these limbs are
held back by
silk threads.

everything
i've become
with my open wounds
and failures,
it's what i dread.

give me a chance
to repair my soul,
give me a new life
so i can break bread.

do this before
the OUTER DARKNESS
takes me whole.

the self is a cruel and tortuous thing.

Eden's Fruit

an apple a day
keeps the demons away,
otherwise i may
want to go out and play,
away from daylight
in the middle of the night
where scary things lurk,
waiting in silence like a crook,
waiting to steal my soul,
then my life will never be whole.

so i better eat my apple today
and stay inside and play,
otherwise i may
fall into the gray.

Sound of Silence

trapped
in the sound
of silence

an echo
of pain
unsung

Quietly,
i retreat
into me.

the unbearable silence eats away at my mind.

A Shakespearean Curse

i'm in permanent mourning
for the death of my future self
because one day i know i'll be dead
buried in a shallow grave with a curse

where you dare not dig
leave my bones alone
just look at my stone
then go back home.

my death will be the glory of my soul.

Willow Trees Weep

welcome to a wild world
where willow trees weep

where sadness reigns supreme
with a silence so deep

everywhere i go
with every little stare
i'm seen as a creep

i wait for the long silence
where i will enjoy my eversleep.

eversleep

['evərslēp]

Noun

1. the state of a troubled or tormented soul, in which it passes from life to death, and whereby it never finds animation in the afterlife

2. the condition of biological death, where the heart and brain are permanently inactive, but the organism's soul remains in a relaxed silence

there is no sweeter death than the first time.

CLOCKWORK

DEATH and TIME —
my two obsessions,
like two hands ticking
in precision, round the clock.

to-morrow, and to-morrow,
but it never comes,
as to-morrow hides time,
it runs with walking shadows.

DEATH and TIME
to-day, and to-morrow
one less, one more,
'til we hit the floor.

DANGER

TIME was ticking
with dagger blades,
ever so sharp,
shining down
on me.

so i went
looking for danger
in dark and muggy places
where people shouldn't be.

FIREBALL

when your love is a fireball
and only one person can catch it,
that's when you know you found the one.

the one
that sets you
on fire!

SERENDIPITY

i always wondered
if serendipity existed
i didn't believe it until
you walked into my life
you were a pleasant surprise
waiting to happen
waiting to arrive
at the perfect time
to brighten up
my darkest days
turn darkness
into light.

Trust In

she said,
"trust in
the nature
of the gods
to relieve of us
of our sins."

that's when
i looked at her
and kissed her on
those pretty little lips.

i seduced her
that very night
and we've paid for
our sins ever since.

TWO STRANGERS

my blood became ice,
cold with pure adrenaline –
crystallized, from outside in.
the moment was eternity
and that's where i still am,
stuck but dancing in bliss,
vibrating in your heartbeat,
perplexed by the universe –
and how two strangers meet,
and how strangers become lovers,
high together – live or die together.

MARIONETTE DOLL

she weaved back and forth,
like a broken MARIONETTE,
controlled by invisible strings,
with her illicit undertones.

imbued with her sexuality
she swept from side to side,
with no skin to hide.

intrigued by her unbidden movements
i watched her closely, all through the night.

you make me want to sin again.

LIVE LIKE YOU'RE DYING

wild, independent and carefree
that is the spirit she possessed
love, peace and grateful joy
she lived each day like she was dying
wise, intelligent and vibrant
she loved like every moment was goodbye.

SOUL OF THE SUN

the soul of the sun is in your hands,
the blood of my heart is in your veins,
when you breathe, i breathe —
and we are one!

Elegant Fire

you dress like elegant fire
with flames that touch my soul
ignite me, light me up!

i finished inside her
as if a black hole swallowed
an exploding supernova.

Icarus

maybe i got too close
to the flames, to the fire,
to my darkest desires.

i saw your beauty
dancing with temptation,
inviting me in.

inviting me to stay,
wanting me to play,
and i did just that.

i am Icarus reborn!

FIREFLIES DANCING

the way we are
is the way i imagine
two fireflies dancing

shining bright
in the beauty of
the midnight sky

traversing over
the currents of
a warm summer breeze

invisible wind
winding through
the stories of our lives

one moment —
a moment forever
captured in space

above time,
no more lies

this truth — sets us free!

LOST CROWNS

we are kings and queens
who lost our crowns

shadowed by a past
that bleeds us dry

we trudge on
with muffled sounds

as we rise
like rockets
in the sky.

BREAKING SKY

i broke for her —
just like the sky breaks
for the passing moon.

Lost

they stood on a perilous edge,
overlooking the city lights,
blinking in the distance.

that's when he said,

"have you ever
pondered the idea
that maybe, just maybe —
no one knows what
is going on in life?
they act like they do, but
deep down they're afraid
and lost in this wilderness
like you and me."

what we search for will never be found.

EDGE OF OBLIVION

i dreamt
the whole fucking world
was burning in flames

and after the ashes settled
all there was was you and me

holding hands,
standing side by side,
at the edge of oblivion.

Darkest Secret

you know
  my darkest
  secret,
  my deepest
  fears,
  all that i hold
  dear.

truly,
  it was fate
  that we met
  right here.

intertwined
  like a weaver's
  basket,
  connected by
  a magical universe.

inside
  your heart
  is a piece
  of my spirit.

BETWEEN HEARTBEATS

for that one moment,
that fraction of a second
between heartbeats,
where silence lives,
she filled a void,
within the gap
that broke
my soul.

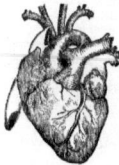

CRAWL

you crawled into my veins
made a home in my heart
pumping the life i need to live
without you i'd be dead.

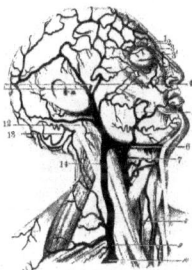

Art of Dying

long ago,
    i mastered
    the art of dying

so i could die
    every day
    in your sweet
    embrace

i poisoned myself
    with the world's
    contagions

so i would
    get sick
    from the life
    we love

everything we do
    gets us one step
    closer to death

a death
    we surely deserve
    from a life
    we spent on dying.

WHEN WINTER CREEPS

when winter creeps
   inside your veins —
   you're ice cold!

you're the lover
   i wanted, but now fear

that's why i bought
   every little thing
   your heart sold

when the leaves fall
   i know the end is near.

WE NEVER BLOOM

we are broken
like the flowers
that never bloom.

our sunshine
lasts a little time
and ends too soon.

our lives
begin to fade
before the first moon.

in warm winds
we blow away
like dust before noon.

My Serenity

i keep spending time
   on dreams that keep dreaming

and i keep picking
   old scabs that keep bleeding

all for the serenity
   of my own suffering.

words are hollow unless you fill them up with meaning.

EVERY RELATIONSHIP

i destroy
every relationship
with the pain of
yesterday.

TIRED BONES

tired bones
   lift me up
   dust me off

find me lost
   in the woods
   to run away

in a land of
   make believe
   and fairy dust

redeem my joy
   like a child
   here to play.

In Dark Silence

there's no bandage big enough for my broken heart,
because the wound she left behind runs deep.

all the places i go and see makes me feel the hurt,
these sad memories never seem to let me sleep.

maybe one day i'll be able to rest in peace,
in dark silence her memories i will keep.

BLOODY THORNS

withered, cracked and worn
   i am not myself in this place.

this soul is abused and torn,
   injustices i fight in this case.

pierced by their hateful scorn,
   what i need is a bit of grace...

but what i get are bloody thorns.

how we bleed shows more of our character
than a thousand words.

SLITTING WRISTS

our romance was
the slit your wrists
kind of love.

a burden
to the soul,
but a blessing
to the senses.

DARKEST DREAMS

one night, the sky turned black
 and never turned back to light.

it was my darkest dreams,
 nightmares coming true.

with every thought —
 i was missing you.

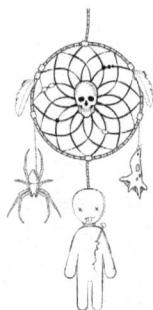

i wake from dreams that are yet to happen.

Unpaid Debt

the debt of our sins
is a millstone around
our necks, dragging us down
into the sea — unquenchable waters
beneath, what we seek is to be free!

DEATH'S TRAGIC COMEDY

i saw DEATH
   laughing outside
   my window sill

"don't worry,
   i'm not coming
   for you quite yet —

your dear loved one,
   next its their life
   i plan to steal.

but when i come,
   i do it swiftly,
   that's a sure bet —

only the hands of time,
   spinning about,
   shall reveal

when you and i meet again,
   that's when i will
   make you forget."

Remember

remember:
   a long time ago

you handed over your scars,
   so i hid them away in the stars

kept safe in the nighttime sky,
never again will you have to cry

remember:
   you bravely let go.

FLAMES IN THE WIND

every single person in this world
that crosses one another's path
crosses their path for a reason.

some are temporary flames,
while others light up your world.

MOST BEAUTIFUL

the most
beautiful thing
in the world
is the thing
barely seen.

COLD SILENCE

there's a moment in time,
    that fades away into silence,
    like a whisper off beautiful lips,
    holding on until it slips.

"think of those you hold dear,
    as the coldness draws near.
    hush my precious friend —
    there's nothing to fear!"

SAD EYES

there is a sadness
    in her eyes.

a faint impression
    in her smile too.

her sadness comes from
    missing something.

unfulfilled wishes that linger
    as tormenting thoughts.

Dead Spaces

life is anything but fair
as we stare into dead spaces
with our wounded heads
holding onto old bandages

we sink into ourselves
as we stare into dead spaces
fading into our thoughts
wishing we were royalty

we waited for the end
as we stared into dead spaces
waiting on a forgiveness
in the winter of our souls.

STARRY NIGHT

she met
   her death
   from a fatal blow

she mirrored
   her fate
   in the stars

her life,
   a flash,
   before she
   had to go.

Changing Seasons

we are winter's solstice,
we are summer's last breath

from season to season
we are consumed by a dying sun
as autumn's leaves greet our death

we bury ourselves in deep white snow,
we die to realize what we did not know.

what if one day all you knew was how to die?

THE END

today,
it ended
in the same place
it began
that night.

where
two lonely souls
intertwined
on hotel sheets
soiled by sin.

he knew
this was the end.

LAY YOU DOWN

i lay you down to die
i lay you down and weep
i lay you down forever
gently you pass into...

eversleep.

THE BEGINNING

he looked down
    at her lifeless face,
more beautiful than ever,
    dressed elegantly
in her rosewood casket.

he spoke softly
    speaking to himself,

"the end of you is
    the beginning of me."

LONELY NIGHTS

these lonely nights, on city streets
leading to the border of timelessness
find me in the middle of nowhere
wishing you were here
wishing i could drive this pain away
with wheels on black asphalt
until midnight turns to gray
and you'd speak my name
one more time, as the sunshine
lights up your eyes.

TOMORROW'S DREAM

tomorrow
    is the first day
    of never more.

a dream,
    a fantasy,
    all imaginary.

SILENT OBLIVION

in between life and death,
waiting for the end to come.

i reserve myself to this demise.

a slow, painful existence
into the SILENT OBLIVION.

there is nothing greater than the whisper
of eternity calling your name.

ETERNITY'S WHISPERS

the whispers
    of eternity
    dance in my ear

as my mind
    decodes secrets
    of infinity

pondering
    what was
    and what will be

in this sea
    of time —
    everlasting.

LONG MOMENTS

when someone dies
you don't have to lose them
for you have all the memories
that can be a light
during your long moments
of suffering.

BLINK

your life is gone in a blink —
gone before you have time to think,
rushing by fast, a blizzard, a blur —
all this commotion, no time for a cure.

sunday school sinners live fast —
go hard, but never do they seem to last,
reach for the sky, for the pretty stars,
all to hide the pain inside, the scars!

soon, we will fade like the stardust,
seeking your love until you rust —
cry your tears, beat your chest,
don't you dare die like the rest!

ALL THERE IS

tomorrow is the disease
the past is a plague
because all there is
and all there ever was
is a moment we call Now.

In My Bones

i feel her
    in the marrow
    of my bones

deep within
    the beating
    of my heart

unconditionally,
    she's given me
    all her love

she's the one woman
    who gave me life
    again and again

from the womb
    through my entire life
    to this very breath

she's the reason —
    i exist.

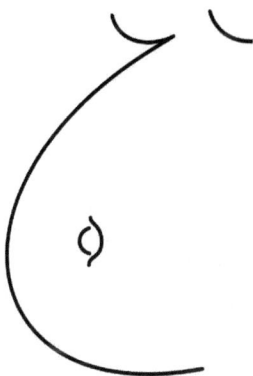

IMMORTALITY

inside the island of (wo)man
sits a spring that leads to
THE IMMORTAL SOUL

A FINAL NOTE

"SOMEBODY should tell us, right at the start of our lives, that we are dying. then we might live life to the limit, every minute of every day. do it! i say. whatever you want to do, do it now. there are only so many tomorrows." — MICHAEL LANDON

RIGHT NOW you are dying. at the start of your life, when you took your first breath, you were dying. you've been dying slowly your entire life. and you never know when your last moment will be. that's why i encourage you to focus on doing the most important things right now. and always make those things your top priority. don't waste your time on meaningless things that don't move you toward your dreams.

dreams conquer death.

FIN

ABOUT THE AUTHOR

At an early age, Alexander Bentley struggled reading words aloud in class. As fortune would have it, he was blessed with a patient mother who spent countless hours working with him after school. The nightly routine paid off and before the school year was over, little Alexander read one hundred small booklets.

His mother's commitment to his literacy skills and development set a firm foundation. It provided Alexander with a proper education, improved his self-esteem, and shaped the course of his life. He now writes poetry – a creative art he embraces wholeheartedly.

But like the many struggles humanity faces on a daily basis, Alexander has long battled his own demons and waged war with dark forces.

In October 2016, Alexander had a medical episode where he fainted after a routine in-office surgery. Within seconds the scene became severe as he stopped breathing and had no pulse. The on-site physician reacted immediately, reviving him to jump-start his heart again. It was in those moments where Alexander felt what was on the other side. He claims, "On the other side is an ancient darkness where light does not exist, and it eagerly wants us to cross over."

Eversleep is a collection of poems that tell the real life experience, through bite-size stories and poetic language, of how the darkness touched Alexander's soul. In November 2016, a few weeks after his medical and spiritual emergency, he submitted a manuscript to the Academy of American Poets for the annual Walt Whitman Award competition.

And even though Alexander did not win that coveted award, he is compelled to share his story with you. He believes that Western society should contemplate death more often, and through the process, we are able to find the real hidden beauty of life.

;

PROJECT SEMICOLON

It's Not Just A Semicolon; It's Hope
It's Inspiration, It's Who. We. Are.

My name is Alexander Bentley, and this is my story. I've carried around with me bottled-up anxiety and self-doubt most of my life, because my early childhood wasn't perfect. Admitting this truth is a difficult task for me, as I tend to mask these feelings of insecurity through my poetry. Sometimes writing poetry brings relief, but other times it doesn't. When I can't find relief through my writing, then my reaction is to find temporary comfort in destructive vices.

It wasn't until this year, in 2017, that I came to the abrupt realization I have been impacted by Adverse Childhood Experiences (ACEs). It's the main reason why certain behaviors, personality traits, and addictions surface. When I experience stress from interpersonal relationships or the weight of daily life, I act out in a negative way. I try to avoid the tension that builds up inside me. My adverse reaction to stressful events is a coping mechanism I learned in childhood.

In my teenage years, I thought about ending my life multiple times. Sadly, thoughts of suicide have also crept into my adult mind. But I hold onto hope. I hold onto the idea that I have a purpose in this life. I want to be known as a great poet and leave a legacy, a memorable impression on the world with my words.

Whatever your hope is; find it with a semicolon, and not the finality of a period. It's only when you have finished your masterpiece, should you be able to find your eversleep. I wish you a long and prosperous life — with many semicolons, in between.

www.projectsemicolon.com

ALEXANDER BENTLEY

Inkslinger. Wordsmith. Poet.

Discover more by the Author on Instagram,
Twitter and other social media outlets.

@abentleywrites